PIONEERS IN HISTORY

BELIEFS AND BELIEVERS

MICHAEL POLLARD

GEC GARRETT EDUCATIONAL CORPORATION

Edited by Rebecca Stefoff

Text © Copyright 1992 by Garrett Educational Corporation
First published in the United States in 1992 by Garrett
Educational Corporation, 130 East Thirteenth Street, Ada,
OK 74820.

Originally published in 1991 by Heinemann Children's
Reference Books, a division of Heinemann Educational
Books. © 1991 Heinemann Educational Books, Ltd.

Manufactured in the United States of America.

Pollard, Michael, 1931-
    Beliefs and believers / Michael Pollard.
        p. cm. — (Pioneers in history)
    Includes index.
    Summary: Describes the major religions of the world
and their founders.
    ISBN 1-56074-037-X
    1. Religions—Juvenile literature.   [1. Religions.]
I. Title. II. Series: Pollard, Michael, 1931-   Pioneers in
history.
BL902.P65   1992
291—dc20   91-36503
                                                          CIP
                                                           AC

Photographic credits

t = top b = bottom r = right l = left

The author and publishers wish to acknowledge, with
thanks, the following photographic sources:

5*t* Michael Holford; 5*b* Camera Press; 6 Sonia Halliday
Photographs; 7 The Bridgeman Art Library; 8 Peter Newark's
Western Americana; 9 Chris Fairclough; 10 Sonia Halliday
Photographs; 11*t* The Bridgeman Art Library; 11*b* John
Rylands Library; 12 Colorific; 13 Camera Press; 14 English
Heritage; 15*t* Sonia Halliday Photographs; 15*b* Chris
Fairclough; 16 Aerofilms; 17 Ronald Sheridan; 18 Colorific;
19*l* Giraudon; 19*r* Sächsische Landesbibliothek; 20 The
Bridgeman Art Library; 21*t* The Mansell Collection;
21*b* Scala; 22*t* J Allan Cash Ltd; 22*b* Crown Copyright
Reserved; 23 Peter Newark's Western Americana; 24 Royal
Geographical Society/Bridgeman Art Library; 25*t* Royal
Geographical Society/Bridgeman Art Library; 25*b* Church
Missionary Society; 26, 27*b* The Church of Jesus Christ
of Latter-Day Saints; 28*t*, 28*b* The Salvation Army;
29 Colorific; 30 Sonia Halliday Photographs; 31 Camera
Press; 33*l* Camera Press; 33*r* Colorific; 34*t* Michael Holford;
34*b* Chris Fairclough; 35 Popperfoto; 36 India Office
Library/British Library; 37*t* Colorific; 37*b* Camera Press;
38*t* Michael Holford; 38*b* Chris Fairclough; 39, 40 Colorific;
41*t* Picturepoint; 41*b* Kyodo News Service; 42 Color Tech,
Mr Graeme Scaife; 43*t* Magnum; 43*b* Chris Fairclough

Cover photographs courtesy of The Bridgeman Art Library
and Michael Holford

Note the reader
In this book there are some words in the text that are printed in **bold** type. This shows that the word is listed
in the glossary on page 46. The glossary gives a brief explanation of words that may be new to you.

Contents

931893

Introduction

Since people first lived on Earth, they have believed in invisible spirits or powers greater than themselves. Their belief in a god or gods gave meaning and direction to their lives.

The world can be a frightening place. People get ill or die young. Crops fail because there is no rain. There are terrible storms, earthquakes, and floods. Wars break out. People suffer from cruelty, poverty, and pain. They feel helpless in the face of such disasters.

Most people need to have faith in some power that is more than human, which can guide and protect them. This belief or faith is called **religion**.

The gods people believed in

Human beings have put their faith in many different kinds of gods. There have been sun gods and rain gods, and gods in the shapes of animals and birds. People have trusted in the spirits of their ancestors.

People's religion shaped the way they lived. At its best, it gave hope and comfort. In inspired men and women to perform brave deeds. Great books and music have resulted from people's beliefs. So have fine buildings and works of art.

▼ Whatever the main religion of a country may be, most countries include people who worship in different ways.

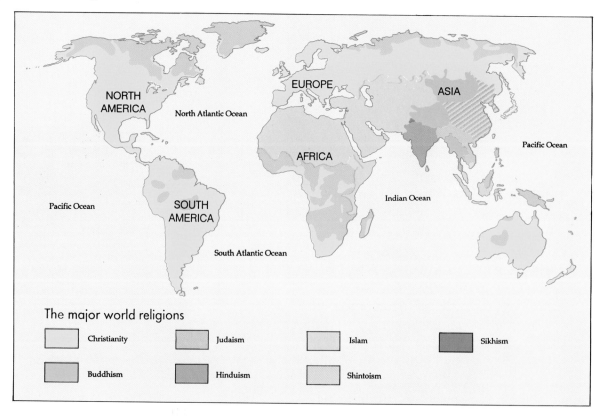

The major world religions

- Christianity
- Judaism
- Islam
- Sikhism
- Buddhism
- Hinduism
- Shintoism

▲ Cats played a part in the religion of ancient Egypt. The Egyptians believed that when a serpent threatened to destroy the sun, a cat bit its head.

Religions of the world

There are many different religions, but most of them fall within five main groups.

Christianity is the religion of about 1000 million people. Christians believe that Jesus of Nazareth was the **Christ**, the son of God. Jesus's teachings, and the story of his life, were written down in the New Testament of the **Bible**.

Islam is the religion of about the same number of people. They are the Muslims, which means "the true believers." Muslims hear God speak through the words of the **Prophet** Mohammed. Their holy book is the **Koran**. Islam means "obedience to God," whom Muslims call Allah.

Hinduism is the religion of about 500 million people, most of them in India. Hindus pray to, or **worship**, many gods. They believe that people's actions in this life lead them to be born again at a higher or lower level in their next life.

Buddhism is another religion of the East. There are about 200 million Buddhists. The **Buddha**, or "one who has seen the light," was an Indian prince called Guatama Siddhartha. His way of understanding life has been taught to his followers ever since.

Judaism is the ancient religion of the Jews. There are about 15 million Jews. They believe in one all-powerful God, and try to obey his laws. The Old Testament of the Bible tells the Jews' story. Jewish beliefs had a great influence on both Christianity and Islam.

Religion and the world

Religious beliefs have done a great deal of good in the world. Most religions teach people to think seriously about their lives and conduct. They teach people to care for others, especially for those in need. However, bad feeling between the followers of different religions has caused endless wars and a great deal of suffering, too.

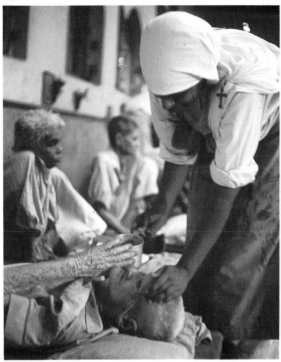

▲ Most religious people feel that it is their duty to help people who are less fortunate than themselves.

5

Moses and the Israelites

The Old Testament of the Bible tells how, long ago, God chose Abraham to be the head of a new nation that would be God's people. Abraham and his family were sheperds and nomads. They lived about 4000 years ago. Abraham's descendants, the Israelites, later settled in Egypt and became slaves of the Egyptians. One of them, called Moses, was to lead his people out of slavery.

The boyhood of Moses

The king of Egypt, the **pharaoh**, worried by the increasing numbers of the slaves, ordered that every newly born male child of the Israelites should be put to death.

Shortly after the pharaoh's order, an Egyptian princess was walking beside the Nile River. She found a baby boy lying in a basket hidden in a bed of reeds. She named him Moses and brought him up.

When Moses grew up, he saw how badly the Egyptians treated the Israelites. In his anger, he killed an Egyptian. After that, Moses escaped from Egypt and went to live in the desert, but God sent him back to help his people.

Out of Egypt

Since the pharaoh would not release the Israelites, Moses decided to take them out of Egypt to a new country that God had

◀ A stained glass window, dating from the 1100s, shows Moses leading the Israelites through the Red Sea.

promised them. He gathered the people together, and they left Egypt in secret. They did not know where they were going, but, according to the Old Testament, God showed them the way. He gave a pillar of fire to follow by night.

The pharaoh sent his army to capture the Israelites and bring them back. Soldiers, in their horse-drawn war chariots, chased the fleeing people to the shores of the Red Sea. The Israelites thought that they would be either captured or drowned, but God saved them. The Old Testament tells that strong winds parted the waters of the Red Sea, and the Israelites crossed on dry land.

The Egyptians were not far behind them, but the wheels of their chariots sank into the sea bed. While they were still struggling, the waters rolled back and drowned them. The Israelites were free at last.

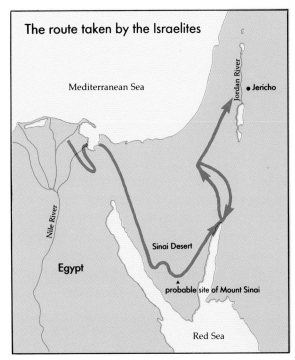

The route taken by the Israelites

Mediterranean Sea

Jordan River

• Jericho

Nile River

Sinai Desert

Egypt

probable site of Mount Sinai

Red Sea

▲ The Israelites wandered in the wilderness for 40 years before they arrived in the Promised Land and captured the city of Jericho.

God's laws

Three months later, when the Israelites reached Mount Sinai, Moses heard God call him to build a place of worship, a **tabernacle**, and gave him a set of laws for the Israelites to follow. The laws God gave to Moses on Mount Sinai are known as the Ten Commandments.

The story of Moses is very important to the Jews. Every year, at the festival of the **Passover**, they recall how the Israelites were led out of slavery into the Promised Land.

◄ The Old Testament tells how God's commandments were written on stone tablets, which Moses received on Mount Sinai.

The search for a homeland

The Jews wished to make their home in the land they believed God had promised them. However, the land was conquered by one empire after another and the Jews were seldom left in peace.

The religion of the Jews centered on their holiest place, the **Temple** in Jerusalem. According to the Old Testament, the Temple was built by King Solomon.

In the year AD 70, the Roman emperor Vespasian ordered the destruction of the Temple. Many Jews were killed or fled in terror. The people of Israel became

scattered, living in countries where they were not always welcome. Often, they met with hatred and cruelly unjust treatment.

For almost 2000 years, they had no homeland. By the 1800s, more than half the Jews in the world were living in Russia. They were not treated like other citizens. They could not move about freely or mix with people who were not Jews. Their homes were often attacked. Many Jews were killed in outbreaks of violence.

Between 1880 and 1920, three million Jews left Russia. Those who could pay the fare sailed for the United States, which welcomed newcomers. Others settled in western Europe. Although the Jews were scattered, they never forgot their religion or their language. They were still the people of Israel.

Hitler and the Jews

In the 1930s, Adolf Hitler came to power in Germany. He blamed the Jews for his country's financial problems, because many of them had become rich and successful. Many people turned against the Jews. Some of the Jews escaped to Britain or the United States, but others were sent to prison camps where they were starved or killed. Then, when Hitler's army

◀ This painting was made in 1938. It shows some of the thousands of Jewish people who fled from persecution in Germany during the 1930s. The man carrying the violin case if the Jewish physicist Albert Einstein. He was born in Germany, but became a US citizen in 1940.

invaded western and eastern Europe, more Jews were sent to their deaths in the prison camps. Six million Jews died before 1945, when the Second World War ended and the killing stopped.

This **persecution** was the worst the Jews had ever known. Many of them felt they would never be safe until they had a country of their own. Although many Jews settled happily in homes around the world after the end of the Second World War, others longed to return to their ancient promised land in Palestine.

The new Israel

In 1918, when Palestine was governed by Britain, the Jews were promised a homeland there. Many Jews went to settle in Palestine, and more followed at the end of the Second World War. In 1948, after much opposition, part of Palestine became the state of Israel.

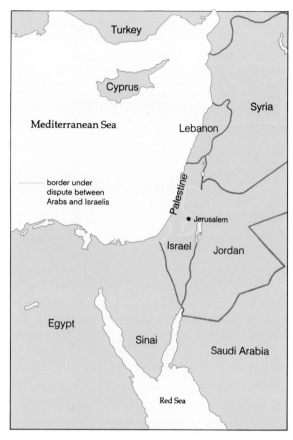

▲ Both the Arab and Israeli people claim to own the land which used to be called Palestine. This argument has led to a series of violent wars.

The opposition came from hundreds of thousands of Arabs who had already made their home in Palestine for hundreds of years. They were angry when their land was given to the Jews. Many Arabs left in despair, to become **refugees** in nearby Arab countries.

Since 1948, there have been four wars between Israel and their Arab neighbors. There is constant bitterness and bloodshed. Over four million Jews now live in Israel, but they cannot live in peace until the quarrel between the Jews and the Arabs is settled.

▲ A Jewish family gathers together each Friday night to celebrate the start of the Jewish Sabbath. On Saturday the family worships at a synagogue, which is the holy building of the Jewish religion. The people hear readings from the holy books of the Jewish faith, the Old Testament and the Torah.

The first Christians

▲ This painting of the baby Jesus in the manger dates from the 1100s. It was painted on the ceiling of St. Martin's church at Zillis in Switzerland.

Jesus Christ was born into a Jewish family in Bethlehem, near Jerusalem, about 2000 year ago. Palestine was then ruled from Rome. It was part of the vast Roman empire that governed all the lands around the Mediterranean Sea.

Jesus worked as a carpenter in the village of Nazareth until he was about 30. At that time, a man called John the Baptist was calling people to turn to God. He **baptized** them in the Jordan River. Jesus was among those who were baptized by John.

Jesus chose 12 men to follow him and be his **disciples**. For three years he went about, preaching to huge crowds of people. He spoke of God as a loving and forgiving father. He healed many people with illnesses who came to him. His disciples believed that he was the Christ, the savior whom the Jews were hoping for.

The Jewish leaders grew angry when they heard people call Jesus "King of the Jews." They plotted to kill him. Pilate, the Roman governor, had Jesus put to death. Jesus was nailed to a wooden cross. He died, asking God to forgive those who killed him, but, according to the New Testament, he rose from the dead into **heaven**. Christians believe that God is in heaven and they wish to be able to enter heaven themselves after they die. They teach that, if they obey God's rules, he will enable them to rise from their own death and join Jesus in heaven.

The first Christians

Jesus chose his disciple Peter to be the founder of the Christian **church**. He did not mean by that just a building in which people could worship. The church of Jesus Christ would be made up of people who believed in him and his teaching.

In the year Jesus died, crowds of people came to Jerusalem for the important Jewish festival of Pentecost. Peter preached to them. He invited them to be baptized as Christians. The first churches started with people baptized that day. They believed, as Christians do still, that Jesus was the son of God and that he would return to Earth. They tried to follow the lessons Christ taught.

It was not easy for the early Christians to meet for worship. Both the Jews and the Romans saw them as trouble makers. Christians were always in danger and had to meet in secret in their own homes.

The church and the world

To begin with, Peter and the other disciples worked among the Jews. Then Peter had a dream. In the dream, God told Peter that the church was not just for Jews, but for people everywhere. The disciples must take the message, or **gospel**, of Christ to the whole world. This meant facing greater dangers.

The man who did most to spread Christianity to other nations was Paul. Brought up as a strict Jew, Paul believed it was his duty to persecute Christians. Then, one day, he heard Christ speak to him. He had a complete change of heart, a **conversion**. After his conversion, Paul spent the rest of his life traveling and preaching the Christian gospel. He was often put in prison, but he would not keep silent. Churches were built in the cities of Asia Minor and Greece, and as far away as Rome.

Finally, Paul was sent to Rome as a prisoner, to go on trial before the emperor. No one knows for certain when he died. Probably both Peter and Paul were put to death in Rome, along with many other Christians, in about AD 64.

▲ This picture was painted in 1497 by the Italian artist Leonardo da Vinci. It is called *The Last Supper*. The painting captures the moment when Jesus tells his followers, or disciples, that one of them will soon betray him.

▼ The four gospels of the New Testament were written within about a hundred years of Jesus's death. They contain everything that is known about his life and teaching. This is part of a fragment of St. John's Gospel. The fragment was found in Egypt, in North Africa, although it is written in Greek.

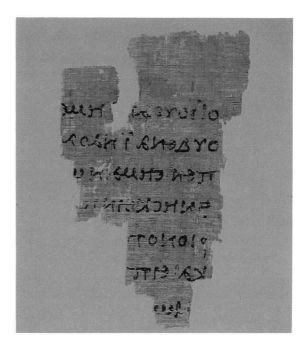

The conversion of the Romans

After Paul's death in Rome, other Christians carried on his work of traveling and preaching. They met and worshipped God in secret, but they refused to worship the same gods as the Romans. The Romans worshipped many different gods and, as time went on, they began to worship their emperors as if they were gods.

Since Christians considered their God to be more important than the Roman emperor, they were regarded as rebels or spies. Their disobedience had to be punished. For 300 years, Christians were badly persecuted. They were tortured, killed, and sent into slavery.

▶ Constantine was the first Roman emperor to believe that his right to rule came from God. These pieces of sculpture were once part of a huge statue of the emperor.

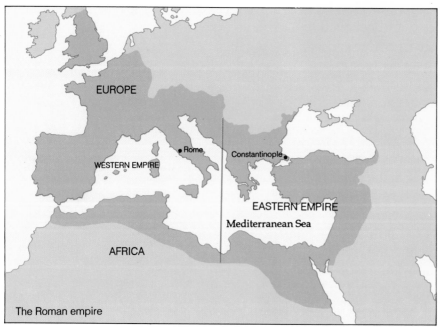

EUROPE

Rome

Constantinople

WESTERN EMPIRE

EASTERN EMPIRE

Mediterranean Sea

AFRICA

The Roman empire

◀ The two halves of the Roman empire became united under Constantine in the year 324.

The flaming cross

The Roman empire became too big to be ruled by one emperor, so it was divided into two parts. In 312, there was a struggle for the leadership of the western empire. The army of Constantine defeated the army of Maxentius in a battle outside Rome. Maxentius was killed, and Constantine became emperor.

It is said that, before the battle, Constantine had a dream. In it, he saw a flaming cross in the sky. Constantine believed this was a sign that the Christians' God was on his side. He ordered his soldiers to carry the Christian cross on their shields and banners. Soon after his victory over Maxentius, he ordered that Christians throughout the empire should be allowed to worship as they pleased.

Constantine was the first Roman emperor to become a Christian. He gave the Christians money to build churches. For the first time, Sunday became a holy day and a day of rest. Constantine took an interest in the work of the churches and encouraged Christians to take part in public affairs.

The new city

In 324, Constantine became emperor of both the eastern and western empires. He built a new city, Constantinople, to be the capital of his Christian empire. He built it at the place where the city of Istanbul now stands. Constantinople became a center of Christian scholarship, as well as capital of the Roman empire.

As Constantine grew older, he believed more and more deeply that Christianity was the true faith. Before he died, he was baptized a Christian. By making Christianity the religion of his vast empire, he made sure that its beliefs would spread throughout the world.

In 1054, the Christian church of the eastern Roman empire came into conflict with the church of the western empire and as a result, the two churches became divided. The church of the eastern empire became the Eastern Orthodox Church. The church of the western empire developed into the Roman **Catholic** Church.

▼ Constantine wanted his new city to be the most magnificent place in the Roman empire. These bronze horses, which are now in Italy, once stood at the gates of Constantinople.

The religious life

Kings and emperors can encourage their followers in one religion or another, but religous faith itself is not about power. It is about the meaning of life. Throughout history, ordinary men and women have found quiet places where they can think, and pray, and try to learn God's will. Often these people own very little. They live in poverty, without money or the comfort of families.

There were religious communities amoung the Jews before the time of Christ. Hindu holy men and Buddhist **monks** have also chosen to live apart from other people in poverty. Their whole lives are given to the religion they have chosen to follow.

Religious communities

About 300 years after the death of Christ, some Christians began to live a life given up entirely to God, a **monastic** life. Some lived alone, but there were also communities of either men (monks) or women (**nuns**).

Monks lived in **monasteries**, and nuns lived in **convents**. Each had its own rules for living the Christian life.

Saint Benedict founded a monastery at Monte Cassino, in Italy, around the year 529. It had its own small church, or **chapel**. His followers ate very little and said prayers at fixed times of the day. Monks and nuns who belonged to the **Order** of St. Benedict were called Benedictines.

Faith and work

Other religous orders sprang up with different rules. Some were devoted to preaching, others to running schools or hospitals, or helping the poor. They offered food and rest to travelers, many of whom were **pilgrims** on their way to visit holy places. Members of religious orders were not allowed to marry. They promised to give everything they had to the church and to obey God. At least four times a day, they went to the chapel to pray.

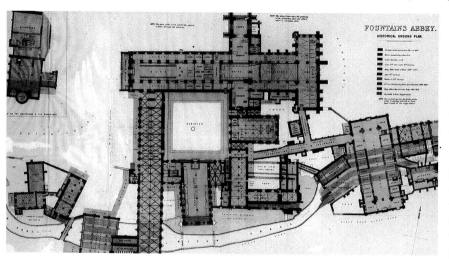

◄ A plan of Fountains Abbey in Yorkshire. Many monasteries were built like this and included a chapel where the monks said their prayers and a cloister where they walked for their recreation.

▲ This stained glass window is in All Saints' Church in the English city of York. It shows members of a religious community obeying Jesus Christ's command to help anyone in need.

Centers of learning

During the Middle Ages, the monks were often the only people in Christian countries who could read and write. The religious orders became centers of learning and had a powerful influence on ordinary people. Young people were educated by members of the religious orders. Many monasteries and convents became rich on the income from their farms, schools, rest-houses, and gifts from pilgrims.

There are still many Christian monks and nuns today. Holy men and women of other religions lead similar lives, though they may live by different rules.

▼ Buddhist monks share a meal in the grounds of a monastery in Tibet.

Holy wars

In the year 610, a prophet in Arabia founded a new religion. This was the Prophet Mohammed, and the religion he founded was Islam. Like the Christians and Jews, his followers, the Muslims, trace their religion back to Abraham. They believe Jesus was a great teacher. Nevertheless, Christians and Muslims regarded each other as enemies. To Muslims, Christians were unbelievers, or **infidels**. Christians described Muslims as people without a religion, or **heathens**.

After the death of Mohammed in 632, the Muslims set out on a holy war to spread Islam to all countries surrounding Arabia, such as Syria and Egypt. In the century after Mohammed began preaching, the Muslims conquered the lands across North Africa to southern Spain in one

▲ The crusaders built fortresses to protect their armies. The Castle of Knights, in Syria, was built by crusaders in 1100, after the first crusade. The castle remained in their possession until it was captured by the Saracens in 1271.

direction and to Palestine, Persia, and the north of India in the opposite direction. Palestine, where Christ had lived, was known to Christians as the Holy Land.

The city of Jerusalem was sacred to both Christians and Muslims. It was both the place where Christ died and where Mohammed was said to have gone up to heaven. For 400 years, Jerusalem belonged to Islam. Then, in 1095, Christian rulers in Europe began a series of holy wars to win control of Jerusalem. They called these wars the crusades.

At first the Christian kings were successful in their war against the Muslims, or **Saracens**, as they called them. Jerusalem was captured in 1099 and became the capital of a Christian kingdom. Then, in 1187, the Saracen warriors, under thier leader Saladin, invaded Jerusalem and seized it back.

The third crusade

When the Christian kings decided to go on a third crusade, soldiers flocked to join their armies. They were sure they were doing God's will. The kings, however, wanted more than just the holy places. They hoped to conquer the Islamic countries such as Palestine for their own power and glory.

The third crusade set out from Europe in 1189. King Richard "the Lionheart" and his army set out from England. He was soon joined by Philip Augustus, king of France, and Frederick Barbarossa, emperor of Germany.

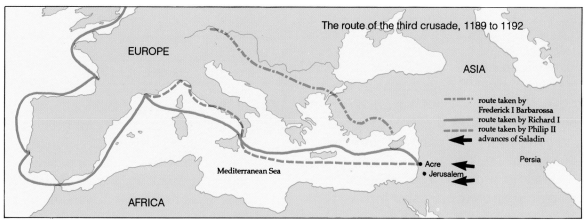

The route of the third crusade, 1189 to 1192

EUROPE

ASIA

route taken by
Frederick I Barbarossa
route taken by Richard I
route taken by Philip II
advances of Saladin

Persia

• Acre
• Jerusalem

Mediterranean Sea

AFRICA

The crusade seemed doomed from the start. Frederick was drowned on the way while he was trying to cross a river. Richard and Philip quarrelled and competed for power against each other. Their armies became divided and many soldiers returned home. Those that remained did not reach the Holy Land until the summer of 1191.

▲ A map of the third crusade, showing the routes taken by Richard the Lionheart, Philip Augustus, and Frederick Barbarossa, and the advances of Saladin.

▼ Saladin was not only a fierce warrior who fought to defend the Islamic faith. He was also a kind leader who encouraged the work of artists and ordered schools and holy buildings to be built.

Jerusalem

Richard had now become the leader of the crusade. He captured the town of Acre and began to march towards Jerusalem. However, he knew by now that his army was no match for the army of Saladin. The third crusade had failed. All Richard could do was try to make peace with the Saracens. Saladin was a just and noble ruler as well as a fine soldier. It was agreed that Christian pilgrims would be allowed to visit Jerusalem, but that Saladin would continue to rule the city.

There were many more crusades during the next hundred years, but the crusaders never achieved their purpose. However, the meeting of soldiers from east and west led to increased trade and the spread of knowledge from one country to another.

The monk from Wittenberg

Christian influence continued to grow until every country in Europe had a Christian ruler. The Catholic church became rich and powerful. Its leader, the **Pope** in Rome, lived like a king. He ruled the church through **bishops**, who were also very rich. Jesus Christ had been a friend of the poor. Many people were disgusted by the greed of the leaders of the church.

In 1513, Pope Leo X needed money to build a huge church in Rome. He raised the money by allowing people to buy forgiveness for their sins. He agreed to grant God's pardon to anyone who could pay for it.

Many ordinary people were deceived by this trickery, but even those who could see that the Pope was wrong were unable to question his authority. However, many priests and scholars were furious at what the Pope had done.

Martin Luther

In October 1517, an incident took place which changed Christianity for ever. A monk went up to the door of a church in Germany and nailed a sheaf of papers to the door. The monk's name was Martin Luther. He was a teacher at the university in Wittenberg. The papers he nailed to the door of the church at Wittenberg were a list of 95 arguments against the sale of pardons. Copies of his statement were printed and sent to all parts of Germany. Luther followed his first protest with further attacks on the Catholic church. He said that Christians should follow Jesus Christ, not the Pope.

Pope Leo was furious. He ordered Luther's books and papers to be burned, and gave him two months to admit that he was wrong. Luther refused. He burned the

◀ St. Peter's Church, in Rome, was built partly with the money Pope Leo X made from the sale of pardons.

Pope's orders expelling him from the Catholic church, in front of a large crowd.

In 1521, the German emperor, Charles V, tried to make peace. He sent for Luther and asked him to admit that he was wrong. Luther could not do that. He felt that he had spoken the truth and that the Bible supported him. "Here I stand. I can do no other, so help me, God," he said.

It was a dangerous stand to take. Martin Luther had angered the emperor as well as the Pope. In 1521, the Pope expelled Martin Luther from the Catholic church. This meant that Luther had to leave the Augustinian order.

▲ A panel from the altarpiece of a church in Wittenberg. The altarpiece shows Martin Luther preaching to his followers and his expulsion from the Catholic church.

A divided church

Luther had many supporters. His demand for reforms in the church led to a movement known as the **Reformation**. Catholics continued to be guided by the Pope. Other Christians joined the Lutheran church, which did not accept the Pope's authority. They were called **Protestants**. Luther translated the Bible into German, so that more people could understand Christ's teaching and think for themselves. The Reformation spread as ordinary people began to question the authority of the Pope.

▲ Martin Luther was a popular preacher. He used words that people could understand and told stories to explain the lessons he wanted to teach.

Soldiers of the church

The Reformation was a great shock to the Catholic church. The Pope and the bishops saw that their church must change, if it wanted to keep the support of its people. They decided to take the message of the church to parts of the world where Christianity was unknown.

New monastic orders were formed, among them the Society of Jesus, whose members were called **Jesuits**. Its founder was a Spanish nobleman and soldier named Ignatius Loyola.

In 1521, when Loyola was 30, he was badly wounded in battle. He had never been religious but, while he was recovering from his wounds, he had a dream, or **vision**, of Mary, the mother of Jesus. From then on, he gave his life to the work of the Catholic church and became a priest.

A new order

The Society of Jesus was founded by Ignatius Loyola in Rome in 1540, with strict rules of discipline for those who joined it. Loyola believed that the church was at war with the world. Jesuits thought of themselves as soldiers of the church.

The Jesuits were expected to obey the Pope without question, just as soldiers obeyed their generals. The Pope and his church could never be wrong.

The Jesuits did not shut themselves away in monasteries as the members of some religious orders did. Instead they became **missionaries** and traveled throughout the world to find new followers for the church.

Jesuit missionaries

A Jesuit missionary called Father Xavier brought many converts to the Society of Jesus. Father Xavier opened churches in India, Sri Lanka, Japan, and China. He would walk through the streets ringing a hand-bell to call people to him. He preached to them in simple songs or chants, which ordinary people could understand. The Jesuits claimed that Father Xavier brought 700,000 people into the church in the ten years before his death in 1552.

▼ Ignatius Loyola was a strict leader. Members of the Society of Jesus who broke the rules did not get a second chance. They had to obey or leave the order.

▶ Francis Xavier was one of the group of seven men who were the first Jesuits. He was the first Jesuit missionary to preach to people in Asia.

Jesuit missionaries also traveled to South America. There, they began to convert the South American Indians.

Jesuits were also at work in Protestant countries. England had officially become Protestant in 1531, so that English families who remained Catholics had to practice their faith in secret. In the reign of Queen Elizabeth I, Jesuit missionaries were searched out and severely punished. Most of them escaped, but one, the English Jesuit Edmund Campion, was arrested, tortured, and tried before being executed in London in 1581.

▶ The years following the Refomation saw fierce conflict between Catholics and Protestants in countries throughout Europe. Followers of each religion persecuted their opponents, and religious books that disagreed with the main religion of a country were burned in public.

Pilgrims in a new land

The Reformation made Christians think deeply about what their religion meant to them. In England, some of them felt that the church had not reformed, or purified, itself enough. These **Puritans** wanted to worship more simply, and live according to the teachings of the New Testament. They disapproved of of riches and of such pleasures as dancing and fine clothes.

Life was difficult for the Puritans in England. They were persecuted and had to worship in secret. One group escaped to the Netherlands, where there was greater religious freedom. Then, after some years, they got permission from King James of England to settle in Virginia, in North America. They hoped to build a new England there, with religious freedom for all. Like the Israelites, they would be pilgrims in a Promised Land.

▲ This copy of the *Mayflower* is anchored at the State Pier in Plymouth, Massachussetts.

▼ The Pilgrims were rowed out to join the *Mayflower* at the English port of Plymouth. During the voyage to North America, two people died and a baby was born.

Saling to a new life

The Puritans returned to England in the late summer of 1620, sailing into the port of Plymouth. There they joined other pilgrims on a ship called the *Mayflower*. On September 16, 1620, the *Mayflower* sailed for North America on the morning tide. There were 102 passengers on board and about 30 sailors.

It was a terrible voyage. The *Mayflower* ran into storms that lasted for days. The ship was blown off course. The food went bad and many of the passengers became ill.

At last, after more than two months, they saw land. The *Mayflower* anchored off Cape Cod, and a group went ashore, thanking God for their safe arrival.

▲ The Pilgrims had permission to land in Virgina. However, the *Mayflower* was not able to reach Virginia, so the Pilgrims landed instead at a place they named Plymouth, after the port they had sailed from in England.

The first Thanksgiving

The Pilgrims built a settlement near their landing place and named it Plymouth. It was to be a place where everyone took an equal part in making decisions. First, they had to build their homes. It was winter and the weather was cold. They had limited supplies of food. Some people were still weak from the long voyage. Sickness spread quickly through the little colony. By spring, half the people had died, and many of the others were too ill to move. They began to think that God had forgotten them.

Then something happened that seemed like a miracle. An American Indian named Samoset visited the colony. He had been sent by his chief, Massassoit, to make friends with the Pilgrims. Samoset taught the Pilgrims how to grow corn and offered to trade with them.

The Pilgrims planted the corn and other seeds they had brought with them, and later reaped a good harvest. The worst times were over. When the harvest was gathered in, the Pilgrims invited the American Indians to share a meal with them, so they could give thanks to God. That was the first Thanksgiving, a feast that is still celebrated in November of every year.

The missionaries

The Jesuits were not the only Christians who traveled overseas to start new churches. As the Protestant churches gained more members, they too sent out missionaries. Many of them went to China, India, and Africa.

The first Europeans to travel into inland areas of Africa were explorers. They brought back stories of dark-skinned people with unfamiliar customs and gods very different from their own. The Christian churches resolved to take the benefits of Christianity to these people.

They felt it was their duty to save the "heathen" from sin and bring them to **salvation**.

One of the most important missionaries was the Scotsman Doctor David Livingstone. He arrived in central Africa in 1840 and spent most of his life there, exploring the country. As well as preaching to the Africans, he tried to defend them from the slave trade. For many years, Africans had been taken from their homes to be sold in foreign countries. Livingstone worked to try to stop this cruel slave trade.

Dangerous journeys

Life was dangerous for the first missionaries. They risked injury from snakes, crocodiles, and lions. They fell ill with mysterious fevers, and many of them died. Yet missionaries succeeded in setting up churches, schools, and hospitals in places where no Europeans had been before.

Missionaries often assumed that Christian beliefs and customs were better in every way than those of other peoples. They persuaded their converts to adopt foreign clothes and manners. However, missionaries like Livingstone had more respect for the Africans' way of life. He tried to help them, not merely preach to them.

◀ David Livingstone was an explorer as well as a missionary. He kept a diary of his travels. Some of the people he met on his journeys had never seen a European before.

▲ It was Livingstone's aim to find a route across Africa by traveling along the Zambezi River. He hoped that this route would attract more traders and settlers to Africa and help stop slavery. Livingstone spent many years exploring possible routes into the middle of Africa that traders could follow.

Missionary work today

Most of the churches founded by the early missionaries in Africa now have African priests and pastors. Some have developed their own styles of worship. The missionaries who work there often teach the people how to grow crops, or give them medical help. Other missionaries preach and teach the Christian gospel just as they always did. However, they must now have the permission of African governments to do their work.

Missionaries still run into danger. They may be caught up in wars and be imprisoned or killed. However, danger does not stop people from doing work they believe God wants them to do.

▲ Foreign missionaries now work under the guidance of the churches of the countries that they visit.

The Mormons

◀ In 1830, Joseph Smith founded the Mormon church in Fayette, New York.

In the early 1800s, a boy named Joseph Smith lived in a small town in upper New York state. When he was about 14 years old, Joseph began to see visions. He said that, in one vision, God and Jesus Christ spoke to him. They told him to get ready to work for them. Joseph said that later an **angel** told him where to find a book written on gold.

Joseph found the book hidden on a hillside. It was written in a strange language, which he translated into English.

The book told the story of three groups of Israelites, who settled in North America about 4000 years ago. The book was written by Mormon, a leader of the tribes. From it grew the Church of Jesus Christ of Latter-day Saints, which is usually called the Mormon Chruch.

The Mormon trail

Joseph Smith began to preach from the Book of Mormon in 1830. For him it was a holy book. Smith and his followers began to go out as missionaries to other parts of the United States.

Soon the Mormons were in trouble. They were different from other Christians in a number of ways. They had no paid priests or ministers, and Mormon men were allowed to marry more than one wife. In Missouri, an angry mob attacked a group of Mormons and killed 17 of them. Joseph Smith and his brother, Hyrum, were killed by a mob on June 27, 1844.

The Mormon Church now had about 5000 members. Under their new leader, Brigham Young, they decided to go west to

▶ The Mormons tried to settle in several towns before they took the Mormon trail that ended in what is now Salt Lake City, Utah.

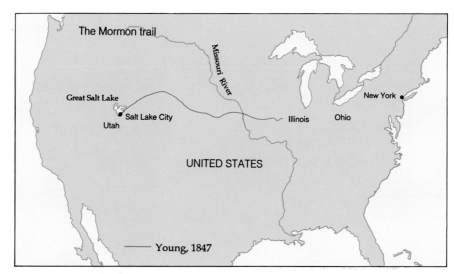

The Mormon trail

Missouri River

Great Salt Lake

Salt Lake City

Utah

New York

Illinois   Ohio

UNITED STATES

—— Young, 1847

escape further persecution. A group of them set out in the spring of 1847, traveling in covered wagons. They took seeds, farming tools, and a year's supply of food. After a long, difficult, and dangerous journey, they reached the Great Salt Lake in Utah. They settled in what is now Salt Lake City, which has been the headquarters of the Mormon Church ever since.

Mormons worldwide

From the start, Mormons believed that it was their duty to tell the rest of the world about the Book of Mormon. They sent their first missionaries to Europe in 1837. Mormons still travel and preach all over the world. There are more than seven million members of their church in many different countries.

Mormons live by a strict set of rules to prepare themselves for the return of Jesus Christ to Earth. They do not smoke or drink tea, coffee, or alcohol. Marriage is encouraged, but men are no longer allowed to have more than one wife.

▲ Many of the people worshipping in this Mormon church are children. Mormons are taught that family life is very important. They believe that they should have as many children as possible.

The Salvation Army

Christians are taught by their religion that it is their duty to help people in pain or in need. A traveling preacher named William Booth felt this duty very deeply when he was living in London in 1864. He was shocked to find so much poverty in such a wealthy city. Few of the churches welcomed poor people, who were often uneducated, dirty, and badly dressed. William Booth decided to do what he could for them.

In 1865, with his wife Catherine, he began a mission of his own in the slums of London. He held meetings wherever he could, in tents, theaters, music halls, or in the streets. These meetings were not solemn like church services. The hymns were sung to cheerful tunes that everyone knew and were played by brass bands.

Booth's work among the poor was so successful that, in 1878, he decided to set up an organization to take the mission into other cities. He called his church the

▲ William Booth, founder and general of the Salvation Army. He traveled all over the world to set up new branches of the Army.

Salvation Army, because he believed that it was fighting a war against evil. Members of the Army wore uniforms and held different ranks to show they were Christian soldiers.

Helping the needy

The members of the Salvation Army did more than preach. They ran hostels where homeless people could stay. They provided meals for anyone who had no money for food. The Salvation Army opened factories where unemployed people, or people newly released from prison, could find work. The Army's message was that everyone, however poor or sinful, was loved by God.

Strong drinks like beer and gin were the cause of much poverty at that time. The alcohol in them helped people to forget their hunger and their cold, damp homes.

▲ This photograph of workers at a London firewood factory dates from the early 1900s. The factory was started by the Salvation Army to give work to people who had no jobs.

However, the money spent on drink should really have been spent on food and clothes.

When Booth preached against the evils of strong drink, the businessmen who made and sold the drinks got angry. They paid gangs to break up Salvation Army meetings. Many members of the Army were hurt in these attacks, but this did not stop their work. They were sure God was on their side.

▼ A Salvation Army parade in Kenya in East Africa. members of the Salvation Army have always held meetings in the streets. People who would never go to a church service sometimes stop to hear something that changes their lives.

The worldwide army

London was not the only city where people lived in poverty. The first branch of the Salvation Army in the United States was opened in Philadelphia, Pennsylvania, in 1880. Soon, there were branches in Canada and Australia. Today, the Army is at work in countries all over the world. The poverty and need are as great as ever.

The Army's message is the same as it was over 100 years ago. People can be saved from evil if they believe in God and lead a Christian life. The Army continues to care for the hungry and homeless, and offers help and advice to anyone in trouble.

Mohammed's vision

The Arabian Desert is a huge area of rock and sand between the Red Sea and the Gulf. For thousands of years, traders have traveled across it from cities like Jerusalem and Damascus, bringing goods to sell at the desert markets. One of these markets was held in the ancient city of Mecca.

In about the year 570, a boy called Mohammed was born in Mecca. His parents died when he was still young, and he found work with the desert trading caravans. When he was 25 he married a rich widow, for whom he undertook several long trading journeys. On his travels he heard Jews and Christians talking about their beliefs. Their faith in one God seemed to him superior to the nature-worship of the people of Mecca.

In 610, when Mohammed was 40, an angel appeared to him in a vision. The angel told him to return to Mecca and preach the true word of God.

▲ Mohammed preaching to his followers. Islam does not allow the face of Mohammed to be shown in pictures. This is why he is shown wearing a veil.

◀ Islam spread quickly in the 120 years after Mohammed's death in 632.

extent of the Islamic world 120 years after the death of Mohammed

▲ The Kaaba stone in the courtyard of the mosque at Mecca. Pilgrims walk around it seven times before they go into the mosque to pray.

Part of what Mohammed preached came from the Bible. However, the angel told him that Jesus Christ had been a great teacher, but not the son of God. There was only one God, Allah, and Mohammed was to be his Prophet. Anyone who believed otherwise would be punished.

The flight to Medina

Mohammed's teaching got him in trouble with the people of Mecca, whose city was already a religious center. Their ancient **shrine**, the Kaaba, was full of images, or **idols** that were being worshipped as gods. Mohammed did not belive that idols should be worshipped, and he wanted them to be destroyed.

To escape the anger of the people of Mecca, Mohammed and his followers fled to a place about 250 miles away. They named it Medina, meaning "the city of the Prophet." The Islamic calendar dates from Mohammed's flight to Medina in 622.

Mohammed's vision

Mohammed became the ruler of Medina and grouped his followers into a strong army. After a few years, they returned to Mecca and captured the city. Mohammed turned Mecca into Islam's holiest city. He continued to preach to his followers. Some of them wrote down the things that had been revealed to him. After Mohammed's death, in the year 632. their writings were put together to make Islam's holy book, the Koran.

The Koran's teaching

The Koran tells Muslims exactly how they should live. There are five main rules, known as the Five Pillars of Islam.

Muslims must declare that there is only one God. They must pray five times a day, starting at dawn, in the **mosque** or wherever they happen to be. Muslims must give one-fortieth of their savings to the poor. They must not eat between sunrise and sunset during the month of fasting, which is called **Ramadan**. They must make the pilgrimage to Mecca once in their lifetime, if they possibly can.

The Koran says that men may have as many as four wives, so long as each wife is fairly treated. It tells Muslims to make war on the infidel, which means anyone who does not accept Islam. Muslims who die in a holy war will be rewarded in heaven.

After Mohammed's death, Islam spread quickly. The Muslims were fierce and fearless warriors who would take any risk, because they were sure that Allah would reward them. Islam was also spread by missionaries who won converts for the religion throughout the world. Today, Islam is the religion of 44 countries.

A divided religion

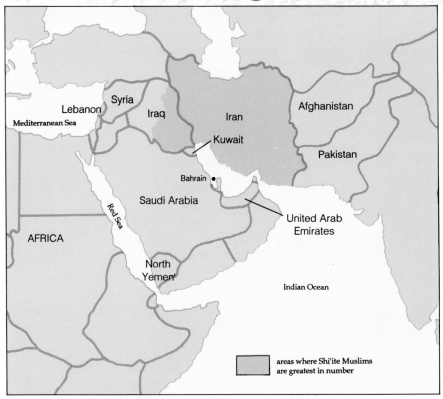

◀ Shi'ites outnumber the Sunnis in Iran, Iraq, Lebanon, and Bahrain. There are also large numbers of Shi'ites in Saudi Arabia, North Yemen, Kuwait, United Arab Emirates, and Syria.

Mohammed was an important teacher and leader. When he died, a quarrel broke out about who should take his place. Mohammed's sons had died young. His daughter Fatima's husband, Ali, said that Mohammed had chosen him to be the new leader of Islam. Mohammed's widow, Ayesha, believed that her father should be her husband's successor, or **caliph**. Many people supported her. They argued that the new leader should be chosen by them all.

Ali lost the argument. Ayesha's father, Abu Bekr, became the first caliph. The following two caliphs were both members of Abu Bekr's family. Then, in 656, Ali took over.

These events split Islam in two. The Muslims who had supported Ali continued to believe that Allah, through Mohammed, had chosen Ali as their leader. This group became known as **Shi'ites**. The Shi'ites word for leader was **imam**. Imam means chosen by Allah, not by the people. Many more Muslims accepted the first three caliphs as the successors of Mohammed. The came be to called **Sunni** Muslims.

When Ali became the imam, a group of his enemies forced an army to fight him. The two sides met near Medina. It is said that Ali's soldiers were winning the battle when soldiers of the other side fixed copies of the Koran to the ends of their spears. The Sunnis were saying that the argument should be settled by the Koran and not by war.

Ali's soldiers did not dare to argue with the Koran. They laid down their weapons and agreed to talk things over. However, the peace between the two sides did not last. Ali was murdered in 661. His death drove the Sunnis and the Shi'ites even further apart. The Shi'ites regarded Ali as another prophet, second only to Mohammed. They believed that he had written down the Koran from Mohammed's teachings. The Sunnis believed that all Muslims were equal in Allah's eyes, and that Ali was no more important that any other Muslim. After Ali's death there was no hope that the two sides would ever agree again.

▲ Shi'ites follow strict rules in the conduct of their lives. A woman must never be seen outside her home without a veil that hides most of her face.

Islam today

The Shi'ites have never forgotten the murder of Ali. This explains why, even today, Shi'ites are ready to die for Allah, as they believe Ali did. Shi'ites keep strictly to the laws laid down in the Koran. They believe that they are the only true believers in Islam.

Throughout the world, only about 15 out of every 100 Muslims are Shi'ites, but in Iran, Iraq, Bahrain, and Lebanon there are more Shi'ites than Sunnis. In 1979, the Shi'ites of Iran led a revolution, which sent the ruler of Iran into exile. The Shi'ites then formed their own strict Islamic state.

▲ Ayatollah Khomeini was the Shi'ite leader who planned the Islamic Revolution in Iran in 1979 and became its spiritual leader.

A religion of many gods

Of all the religions in the world, Hinduism is perhaps the most complex. Hinduism means "the religion of Hind," or India. There is no fixed set of rules. Hindus have no great leader like Mohammed or Jesus Christ whose teachings were passed on to guide their followers.

Hinduism is a mixture of beliefs, some from India and some from the Aryan people who invaded India about 3500 years ago.

Some Hindus have such respect for life that they will not kill any living creature. Others are more warlike and will fight to defend their religion.

Most of the 500 million Hindus in the world live in India, but Hindus who have settled in other countries have taken their religion with them.

▲ Images of Shiva, the Hindu god of life, show him in many different ways. This bronze image shows him as "Lord of the Dance."

◀ Diwali is an important Hindu festival which takes place every year and lasts for five days. During the festival, Hindu families light lamps in honor of the god Rama.

The Hindu gods

To Hindus, all of life belongs to the gods, and the gods are everywhere. There are three main gods. Brahma made the world, Vishnu rules it, and Shiva gives life and can take it away. Hindus also worship gods who are related to the three main gods. Each Hindu family and village has its own gods, which they worship. Hindus have places in their homes called shrines that are dedicated to the gods. Hindus pray at these shrines every day, and offer gifts to the gods.

A place in life

Most Hindus believe that if you do good deeds in this life you will be born again into a better class in society. If you do bad deeds, you may be born again as a worm or a pig. Your place in life is the result of your actions in a previous life. Every Hindu family belongs to a certain class in society, or **caste**. The people of one caste often do the same kind of work. They live apart from members of other castes, and mix with them as little as possible. Hindus cannot move from one caste to another. A person's caste never changes.

The lowest caste of all is that of the "untouchable." They are the poorest people and do the dirtiest work. They may have to beg for a living.

Mohandas Gandhi

One of the most important Hindus of recent times was Mahandas Gandhi, called "The Mahatma," or great soul. He was a wise spiritual and political leader, who fought for justice but refused to use violence. He struggled to improve conditions for the untouchables and to break the caste system. He spent most of his life working for Indian freedom from British rule. He died in 1948, the year in which independence was granted.

▶ Gandhi believed in living simply. He wove the material to make the clothes he wore and had very few possessions. He is shown here in 1931 in London after a meeting with the British prime minister, Ramsey MacDonald.

Nanak and his followers

In 1469, a Hindu boy called Nanak was born in the Punjab, in northwestern India. His father and grandfather were teachers of religion, or **gurus**. When Nanak grew up, he too became a guru. However, he thought that some Hindu ideas, especially their ideas of caste, were wrong. He believed people should have the right to make the best of their lives. They should not have to accept the caste into which they were born.

Nanak lived at a time when India was invaded by Islamic armies from the west. He grew interested in the beliefs of the Muslims and found that many of them appealed to him. In Islam, there was one supreme God. All men and women had an equal chance to receive God's blessings. This was not what Hindus believed.

Nanak began to teach that people of all religions should live in peace with one another. He said that the Hindu caste system was wrong. He welcomed the people who came to hear him, whatever their caste. Nanak called them his followers, or **sikhs**. He wandered all over India preaching, often chanting hymns to get his message across to the people.

The Sikhs' Golden Temple

Before Nanak died in 1539, he appointed a new guru for the Sikhs, who was called Angad. When Angad's period of leadership was over, a new guru, Amar Das, took over, and so on. From 1556 to 1605, Emperor Akbar was the Muslim ruler of the Moghul empire, which stretched from Afghanistan across northern India. Akbar believed, as Nanak had, that all religions were worthy of respect. He gave the Sikhs land on which to build a temple. One-tenth of each Sikh's income was collected to pay for the building.

The fifth guru, Arjun Mal, started to build the Golden Temple in 1581. It became a place where worshippers could mix freely, whatever their caste. The pool of Amritsar, in front of the temple, gave its name to the city that grew up around it.

◄ Nanak was born at Talwandi, near Lahore in the Punjab region of northern India. He believed there should be no division between the Muslims and Hindus.

▲ The Golden Temple at Amritsar.

The Muslim emperors, Jehangir and Shah Jehan, who followed Akbar began to persecute the Sikhs. Then, from about the 1730s, the power of the Moghul empire began to be weakened. Afghans from the north invaded India and attacked the Golden Temple. Parts of it were destroyed in 1757 and again in 1762. Each time it was rebuilt by the Sikhs until in 1764, the Afghans blew up the temple.

The Sikhs go to war

In the 200 years since Nanak's death the Sikhs had become almost a separate nation, with their own style of writing and dress. They had begun as a peaceful people, but they had learned how to fight for their religion. The Sikhs went to war and drove back the Afghans.

In 1765, they began to rebuild the Golden Temple. This is the one that still stands in Amritsar today. The outside walls are made of marble. The upper walls and dome shine with gold leaf. For Sikhs it is the holiest place in the world. Today, the Golden Temple has become a center of conflict once again, this time between the Indian government and the Sikhs.

▼ Sikh men all wear turbans. Their religion forbids them to cut their hair, smoke, or drink alcohol.

The Buddha

About 2500 years ago, a son was born to the prince of a warrior tribe living in the country in southern Asia that is now called Nepal. His name was Gautama Siddhartha. His family were Hindus.

Siddhartha was brought up in his father's luxurious palace, and studied with many of the Hindu teachers of that time. When he was 16, he married a princess, who later gave birth to a son.

Soon after the birth of his child, Siddhartha came into direct contact with the sufferings of the world. While being driven through the city, he saw for himself how hard life was for most people outside the palace. Siddhartha was changed for ever by what he saw. He no longer felt able to live the comfortable life into which he had been born. What was the use of life, he wondered, when so many people were poor, sick, or dying? So, at the age of 29, Siddhartha left his wife and son, and went wandering through India, searching for an answer to this difficult question.

▲ Buddha is usually shown sitting cross-legged, with a straight back and his hands in his lap. Buddhists use this position for meditation.

◄ Buddhism began in India and its ideas were soon spread throughout Asia and China by followers of the Buddha. These Buddhist monks belong to a monastery in Hong Kong.

What Buddhists believe

One day, many years later, he was sitting under a fig tree when the answer came to him. It filled him with happiness. Siddhartha realized that the answer to the meaning of life was within everyone, not just within himself. This led Siddhartha to believe that people should not complain if they suffered poverty or sickness. They should accept life as it was. One day they would find happiness and peace that is called **nirvana**. Siddhartha believed that this joyful state was within the reach of everyone.

Siddhartha began to teach other people what he had discovered. He called himself the Buddha, which means "one who has found the truth." He sent his first followers out to teach his beliefs to others. Soon, Buddhism spread through India to Sri Lanka, China, and the countries of Southeast Asia.

Man or god?

No one wrote down the things Buddha taught while he was alive. After he died, his followers kept his ideas alive by their preaching. As the teachings of the Buddha were passed on from one group to another, they changed. Some ideas seemed more important to one group than to another. As it spread, Buddhism developed in slightly different ways in different countries.

All Buddhists believe that they should spend part of every day thinking about the meaning of life, as Buddha did. Some set aside a special time to **meditate**. Others believe that they can think just as deeply as they go about their everyday life. Some Buddhists go to temples to meditate in front of a statue of the Buddha. Others meditate in their own homes. All followers of the Buddhist faith believe that the Buddha was an important teacher. Some think of him as a god.

▶ In recent years, the teachings of Buddhism have spread out from Asia. Buddhist communities have been set up in parts of the United States and western Europe.

The emperor and the sun goddess

There is a religion in Japan which belongs only to the Japanese. It began nearly 2000 years ago, when the ruling people were sun-worshippers. They believe that their king, Jimmu, was the direct descendant of the goddess of the Sun. These people believed in many nature gods and spirits, much as the Romans did. The religion of the sun-worshippers came to be called "the way of the gods," or **Shintoism**.

Jimmu became the first emperor of Japan, and every Japanese emperor since that time is believed to have been descended from him, right down to the present day. Until 1945, followers of Shinto believed that every emperor was a god, rather than being just the descendent of a god like everyone else. In that year, Emperor Hirohito announced that he did not wish to be thought of as a god.

The idea that human beings are the children of gods is important in Shintoism. Followers of the Shinto religion worship their ancestors, believing that their line of descent from the gods is unbroken. In turn, they believe that their descendants will worship them in the future.

When the goddess of the Sun sent Jimmu to Earth, he is said to have brought with him a mirror, a sword, and a jewel. To this day, Shinto shrines contain mirrors, swords, and jewels to remind them of this story.

◀ The Shinto festival of Shichi-Go-San is celebrated on November 15 each year. Schichi-Go-San means "seven-five-three." It is a festival for girls aged seven. boys aged five, and three-year-olds of both sexes. Parents take their children to the shrine in their best clothes and thank the gods for their children's good health.

Shintoism and Buddhism

The Shinto holy books tell stories, but they do not lay down any rules about the way people should live. The job of Shinto priests is to act as messengers between people and the gods, not to tell people what the gods want. The priesthood passes from father to son, so a priest does not choose his profession.

About 1400 years ago, Buddhism reached Japan. At first, many people were opposed to the new religion, but soon the followers of Buddhism and of Shintoism were living happily side by side. Unlike Buddhism, Shintoism is a national religion. No one has ever tried to make converts outside Japan. Today, many Japanese follow both religions. Nine out of ten weddings in Japan take place in Shinto shrines. The same people might choose to have a Buddhist funeral when they die, because Buddhists believe that life goes on after death.

▼ Shinto is a religion of the family, and a wedding is a great occasion.

▲ The New Year is Japan's most important holiday. During the New Year festival, lucky symbols like these Daruma dolls are very popular. When each doll is bought, it has no eyes. The person who buys it makes a wish and if the wish comes true, eyes are painted on to the doll's face.

A Shinto shrine

Shinto shrines are often very beautiful. Outside every Shinto shrine there is a wooden gateway with a basin of water beside it. Worshippers must be clean before they enter. After rinsing their mouths and fingers, they walk under a straw rope strung between two posts. This stops evil spirits entering the shrine.

There is no formal religious service or teaching, as there would be in a Christian church or an Islamic mosque. Shinto worshippers stand before a white silk curtain, bow, clap their hands and say their prayers silently. They may leave cakes, glasses of wine, or small gifts of money for the gods. There is a place in front of the shrine where they leave written messages for the gods.

New religions

What does life mean? What are we all doing on Earth? What will happen to us when we die? People today still ask these questions, just as they did thousands of years ago. Some of them find answers in the religions of the past. Others look for new faiths. The Baha'i and Rastafarian faiths are two of the newer religions.

A new prophet

The Baha'i faith arose about 150 years ago in Iran. A man known as Baha'u'llah, or "Glory of God," said that God had sent him to bring religion up to date. He taught that people of all religions worship the same god. Each new religion was another step nearer to the truth about life.

Baha'u'llah was persecuted by the rulers of Iran. He and his followers were thrown into prison and sent into exile. Soon after Baha'u'llah's death in 1892, Baha'is traveled to the United States to help spread their religion. Since then, the Baha'i faith has found followers in most countries.

There are about five million Baha'is in the world today. The tomb of Baha'u'llah in the Israeli town of 'Akka is their most sacred shrine. Baha'is believe that there is one God, although followers of different religions call him by different names. They believe that he loves all people in the world equally and that the whole world is one country.

Baha'is teach that the people of all religions should live in peace, and that men and women should have equal rights. The Baha'is have no priests. In some countries, they still suffer persecution and even death for their beliefs.

◀ The Baha'i faith has members in almost every country of the world. This Baha'i House of Worship is in New Delhi, in India.

▲ Haile Selassie I, or Ras Tafari, in his uniform as Emperor of Ethiopia. Rastas believe that he is God in a human form and that he is still alive.

The Lion of Judah

Ras Tafari, who was also called Haile Selassie I, was the Emperor of Abyssinia from 1930 to 1974. "The Lion of Judah" and "King of Kings" were two of his titles, chosen to show that he was descended from King Solomon, the Old Testament king who built the Temple in Jerusalem.

Rastas, or Rastafarians, believe that the coming of Ras Tafari was written in the Bible. For them, the Old Testament is the story of black people. They were the Chosen People of a black god. The Promised Land they were led to was Abyssinia, now called Ethiopia. Then, much later, they were taken as slaves to the West Indies and the United States. They believe that, one day, they will return to Abyssinia, where Ras Tafari will be waiting to welcome them.

The Rastafarian movement began on the island of Jamiaca. The prophet of the movement was Marcus Garvey, a Jamaican, who preached that all black people should unite together in their own country with their own government. When Jamaicans emigrate to other countries, they take their beliefs with them.

Rastas believe that it is more important to obey God's law written in the Bible than to obey the law of the land, and this can bring them into conflict with the police. Believers today find it as difficult as it ever was to follow both the rules of their religion and those of the land in which they live.

▲ Reggae is the music of the Rastas. Drumming is an important part of reggae music. The words of reggae songs tell the story of Rasta beliefs.

Time chart

Date	Eruope, Australia, New Zealand	Asia	Africa	North, Central, and South America
BC				
1900		Life of Abraham		
1280 – 1250		The flight of the Isrealites from Egypt into the Promised Land		
483		Death of Siddhartha (Buddha)		
AD				
30		Crucifixion of Jesus Christ		
64	Execution of St. Paul in Rome			
312	Constantine becomes western emperor of Rome			
324	Constantine becomes emperor of the whole Roman empire			
529	St Benedict founds the Monte Cassino monastery			
538		Introduction of Buddhism to Japan		
543	Death of St. Benedict			
610		Mohammed's vision		
632		Death of Mohammed		
656		Ali becomes leader of Islam		
661		Murder of Ali		
1054	Separation of the Eastern Orthodox church and the Roman Catholic church			
1096	Start of the first crusade			
1187	Saladin captures Jerusalem			
1189	Start of the third crusade			
1513	Leo X becomes Pope			
1517	Martin Luther nails his 95 Theses to the door of a church in Wittenberg			

Date	Eruope, Australia, New Zealand	Asia	Africa	North, Central, and South America
1534	Henry VIII appoints himself Supreme Head of the Church of England and breaks away from the Church of Rome			
1534	St. Ignatius Loyola founds the Society of Jesus			
1546	Death of Martin Luther			
1547	Death of Henry VIII			
1556	Death of St. Ignatius Loyola			
1581		The building of the Sikh Golden Temple begins		
1620				The Pilgrims sail to North America
1830				Joseph Smith founds the Mormon Church
1840			David Livingstone arrives in Africa	
1844				Murder of Joseph Smith
1847				The Mormon trail to Salt Lake City
1865	William Booth starts his first London mission			
1873			Death of David Livingstone in Africa	
1877	William Booth founds the Salvation Army			
1892		Death of Baha'u'llah		
1912	Death of William Booth			
1930			Ras Tafari (Haile Selassie) becomes Emperor of Ethiopia	
1948		First Arab-Israeli war		
1967		Six Day war between the Arabs and Israelis		
1973		Fourth Arab-Israeli war		
1979		Islamic Revolution in Iran		
1989		Death of Ayotollah Khomeini, Shi'ite leader of the Islamic Revolution		

Glossary

angel: a messenger from God, often shown as a human being with wings

Baha'i: the religion founded by Baha'u'llah

baptize: to dip into water as a sign of entry into the Christian church

Bible: the holy books of Jews and Christians; the Old Testament books include the history and laws of the Jews; the New Testament tells the story of Jesus's life and death, and of how the Christian church began

bishop: the highest order of priests in the Christian church

Buddha: the title given to Gautama Siddhartha, meaning a person of great wisdom and virtue

Buddhism: the religion founded by Buddha

caliph: a leader and defender of the Islamic faith

caste: a level or class in Hindu society

Catholic: the part of the Christian religion which is led by the Pope

chapel: a small church, or part of a larger one

Christ: the one specially sent by God

Christianity: the religion of Chrisitans. They live their lives by following the teachings of Jesus Christ

church: (1) all Christians (2) a particular group of Christians (3) a building for Christian worship

convent: the place where a religious community of women lives

conversion: the change from one religion to another, or to a particular belief from unbelief. The person who changes is a convert

disciple: the follower of a teacher or religious leader

gospel: a word meaning good news which is used to describe the written account of Christ's life and teachings

guru: a religious or spiritual teacher

heathen: a person without religion or without a particular religion

heaven: the place where God is. Heaven is also thought of as a place of joy

Hinduism: a religion that is based on more than one god, and a belief in rebirth. Hindus believe that the way people live in one life affects the sort of life they will be reborn into

idol: an image set up for people to worship

imam: an Islamic leader, chosen by God

infidel: someone who does not believe in Islam

Islam: the religion which is based on the teazchings of the Prophet Mohammed. Followers of Islam are called Muslims

Jesuit: a member of the Society of Jesus

Judaism: the faith and practice of the Jewish people

Koran: the holy book of Islam

meditate: to think deeply and in silence

missionary: someone who travels the world teaching others about religion

monastery: the place where a religious order of men lives

monastic: a word that describes a simple, prayerful way of life, such as is lived in monasteries

monk: a man who has joined a religious order

mosque: an Islamic place of worship

nirvana: a state of perfect place and happiness

nun: a woman who has joined a religious order

order: a community of religious people such as nuns or monks who live together and follow certain rules about how to live

Passover: a time when Jews remember their escape from Egypt

persecution: the cruel treatment of a group of people

pharaoh: a ruler in ancient Egypt

pilgrim: a person traveling for religious reasons

Pope: the bishop of Rome, who is head of the Catholic church

prophet: someone who brings God's message to people

Protestant: a member of the part of the Christian church that does not accept the Pope as its leader

Puritans: English Protestants who wanted to worship more simply

Ramadan: the ninth month of the Muslim calendar, when Muslims do not eat or drink during daylight hours

Rastafarian: a follower of the religion founded by Ras Tafari

Reformation: the movement of change in the Christian church started by Martin Luther's protest against the Pope

refugee: a person who is forced to leave his or her own country

religion: a belief in a god, or in many gods and spirits

saint: a holy person

salvation: the saving of a person's soul by God

Saracen: the name used for any Arab or Muslim at the time of the Crusades

Shi'ite: the Islamic group which believes that Ali, Mohammed's son-in-law, was the first true caliph

Shintoism: the Japanese religion which worships nature and ancestors

shrine: a place sacred to a particular god or saint

Sikh: a follower of Sikhism, the religion founded by Nanak

Sunni: the Islamic group that believes that Muslims had the right to choose Abu Bekr as the first caliph

tabernacle: a tent used for worship

temple: a building used for worship

vision: a kind of dream, often of gods or angels

worship: prayers and praise offered to a god or gods

Index